LE CORBEAU
EDITION BILINGUE ILLUSTREE : FRANÇAIS / ANGLAIS

POËME PAR EDGAR POE

TRADUCTION FRANÇAISE DE STÉPHANE MALLARMÉ

AVEC ILLUSTRATIONS PAR ÉDOUARD MANET

A partir de l'Edition

1875

Enrichi par les Illustrations de Gustave Doré,

A partir de l'Edition Américaine, 1884

Copyright © 2018 Barry

All rights reserved.

ISBN: 9781729262368

TABLE DES MATIERES

LE CORBEAU / THE RAVEN 1

ILLUSTRATIONS PAR GUSTAVE DORE 27

Illustration 1 Title-page, designed by Elihu Vedder._____27
Illustration 2 "Nevermore."_____28
Illustration 3 ANANKE._____29
Illustration 4 "Once upon a midnight dreary, while I pondered, weak and weary, Over many a quaint and curious volume of forgotten lore."_____30
Illustration 5 "Ah, distinctly I remember it was in the bleak December, And each separate dying ember wrought its ghost upon the floor."_____31
Illustration 6 "Eagerly I wished the morrow;—vainly I had sought to borrow From my books surcease of sorrow— sorrow for the lost Lenore."_____32
Illustration 7 "Sorrow for the lost Lenore."_____33
Illustration 8 "For the rare and radiant maiden whom the angels name Lenore— Nameless here for evermore."__34
Illustration 9 "'T is some visiter entreating entrance at my chamber door— Some late visiter entreating entrance at my chamber door."_____35
Illustration 10 "Here I opened wide the door;— Darkness there, and nothing more."_____36

Illustration 11 "Doubting, dreaming dreams no mortal ever dared to dream before." 37

Illustration 12 "'Surely,' said I, 'surely that is something at my window lattice; Let me see, then, what thereat is, and this mystery explore.'" 38

Illustration 13 "Open here I flung the shutter." 39

Illustration 14. "A stately Raven of the saintly days of yore. Not the least obeisance made he; not a minute stopped or stayed he." 40

Illustration 15 "Perched upon a bust of Pallas just above my chamber door— Perched, and sat, and nothing more." 41

Illustration 16 "Wandering from the Nightly shore." 42

Illustration 17 "Till I scarcely more than muttered, 'Other friends have flown before— On the morrow he will leave me, as my hopes have flown before.'" 43

Illustration 18 "Then, upon the velvet sinking, I betook myself to linking Fancy unto fancy." 44

Illustration 19 "But whose velvet violet lining with the lamplight gloating o'er 45

Illustration 20 "'Wretch,' I cried, 'thy God hath lent thee— by these angels he hath sent thee Respite—respite and nepenthe from thy memories of Lenore!'" 46

Illustration 21 "On this home by Horror haunted." 47

Illustration 22 . . . . "Tell me truly, I implore— Is there—is there balm in Gilead?—tell me—tell me, I implore!" 48

Illustration 23 "Tell this soul with sorrow laden if, within the distant Aidenn, It shall clasp a sainted maiden whom the angels name Lenore." _____ 49

Illustration 24 "'Be that word our sign of parting, bird or fiend!' I shrieked, upstarting." _____ 50

Illustration 25 "'Get thee back into the tempest and the Night's Plutonian shore!'" _____ 51

Illustration 26 "And my soul from out that shadow that lies floating on the floor Shall be lifted—nevermore!" _____ 52

Illustration 27 The secret of the Sphinx. _____ 53

LE CORBEAU / THE RAVEN

ILLUSTRATIONS PAR ÉDOUARD MANET

Once upon a midnight dreary, while I pondered, weak and weary,

Over many a quaint and curious volume of forgotten lore—

While I nodded, nearly napping, suddenly there came a tapping,

As of some one gently rapping—rapping at my chamber door.

"'Tis some visitor," I muttered, "tapping at my chamber door—

                Only this and nothing more."

Une fois, par un minuit lugubre, tandis que je m'appesantissais, faible et fatigué,

Sur maint curieux et bizarre volume de savoir oublié—

Tandis que je dodelinais la tête, somnolant presque: soudain se fit un heurt,

Comme de quelqu'un frappant doucement, frappant à la porte de ma chambre—

                    Cela seul et rien de plus.

Ah, distinctly I remember, it was in the bleak December,

And each separate dying ember wrought its ghost upon the floor.

Eagerly I wished the morrow;—vainly I had sought to borrow

From my books surcease of sorrow—sorrow for the lost Lenore—

For the rare and radiant maiden whom the angels name Lenore—

                    Nameless here for evermore.

Ah! distinctement je me souviens que c'était en le glacial Décembre,

Et chaque tison, mourant isolé, ouvrageait son spectre sur le sol.

Ardemment je souhaitais le jour—vainement j'avais cherché

D'emprunter à mes livres un sursis au chagrin—au chagrin de la Lénore perdue—

De la rare et rayonnante jeune fille que les anges nomment Lénore:—

De nom pour elle ici, non, jamais plus !

And the silken sad uncertain rustling of each purple curtain

Thrilled me—filled me with fantastic terrors never felt before;

So that now, to still the beating of my heart, I stood repeating

"'Tis some visitor entreating entrance at my chamber door—

Some late visitor entreating entrance at my chamber door;—

This it is and nothing more."

Et de la soie l'incertain et triste bruissement en chaque rideau purpural

Me traversait—m'emplissait de fantastiques terreurs pas senties encore:

Si bien que, pour calmer le battement de mon cœur, je demeurais maintenant à répéter

« C'est quelque visiteur qui sollicite l'entrée, à la porte de ma chambre—

Quelque visiteur qui sollicite l'entrée, à la porte de ma chambre; —

C'est cela et rien de plus. »

Presently my soul grew stronger; hesitating then no longer,

"Sir," said I, "or Madam, truly your forgiveness I implore;

But the fact is I was napping, and so gently you came rapping,

And so faintly you came tapping—tapping at my chamber door,

That I scarce was sure I heard you"—here I opened wide the door:—

                Darkness there and nothing more.

Mon âme devint subitement plus forte et, n'hésitant davantage

« Monsieur, » dis-je, « ou Madame, j'implore véritablement votre pardon;

Mais le fait est que je somnolais et vous vîntes si doucement frapper,

Et si faiblement vous vîntes heurter, heurter à la porte de ma chambre,

Que j'étais à peine sûr de vous avoir entendu. »—Ici j'ouvris, grande, la porte: —

                Les ténèbres et rien de plus. »

Deep into that darkness peering, long I stood there wondering, fearing,

Doubting, dreaming dreams no mortal ever dared to dream before;

But the silence was unbroken, and the stillness gave no token,

And the only word there spoken was the whispered word, "Lenore!"

This I whispered, and an echo murmured back the word, "Lenore!"—

                        Merely this and nothing more.

Loin dans l'ombre regardant, je me tins longtemps

A douter, m'étonner et craindre, à rêver des rêves qu'aucun mortel n'avait osé rêver encore;

Mais le silence ne se rompit point et la quiétude ne donna de signe:

Et le seul mot qui se dit, fut le mot chuchoté « Lénore! »

Je le chuchotai—et un écho murmura de retour le mot « Lénore! »—

> *Purement cela et rien de plus.*

Back into the chamber turning, all my soul within me burning,

Soon again I heard a tapping, somewhat louder than before,

"Surely," said I, "surely that is something at my window lattice;

Let me see, then, what thereat is, and this mystery explore—

Let my heart be still a moment, and this mystery explore;—

'Tis the wind and nothing more."

Rentrant dans la chambre, toute mon âme en feu,

J'entendis bientôt un heurt en quelque sorte plus fort qu'auparavant.

« Sûrement, dis-je, sûrement c'est quelque chose à la persienne de ma fenêtre ;

Voyons donc ce qu'il y a et explorons ce mystère—

Que mon cœur se calme un moment et explore ce mystère; —

« C'est le vent et rien de plus. »

Open here I flung the shutter, when, with many a flirt and flutter,

In there stepped a stately Raven of the saintly days of yore.

Not the least obeisance made he; not an instant stopped or stayed he;

But, with mien of lord and lady, perched above my chamber door—

Perched upon a bust of Pallas just above my chamber door—

        Perched and sat and nothing more.

Au large je poussai le volet; quand, avec maints enjouement et agitation d'ailes,

Entra un majestueux Corbeau des saints jours de jadis.

Il ne fit pas la moindre révérence, il ne s'arrêta ni n'hésita un instant:

Mais, avec une mine de lord ou de lady, se percha au-dessus de la porte de ma chambre—

Se percha sur un buste de Pallas juste au-dessus de la porte de ma chambre—

        Se percha, siégea et rien de plus.

Then this ebony bird beguiling my sad fancy into smiling,

By the grave and stern decorum of the countenance it wore,

"Though thy crest be shorn and shaven, thou," I said, "art sure no craven,

Ghastly grim and ancient Raven wandering from the Nightly shore—

Tell me what thy lordly name is on the Night's Plutonian shore!"

                      Quoth the Raven, "Nevermore."

Alors cet oiseau d'ébène induisant ma triste imagination au sourire,

Par le grave et sévère décorum de la contenance qu'il eut:

« Quoique ta crête soit chue et rase, non! dis-je, tu n'es pas pour sûr un poltron,

Spectral, lugubre et ancien Corbeau, errant loin du rivage de Nuit—

Dis-moi quel est ton nom seigneurial au rivage plutonien de Nuit. »

                  Le Corbeau dit: « Jamais plus. »

Much I marvelled this ungainly fowl to hear discourse so plainly,

Though its answer little meaning—little relevancy bore;

For we cannot help agreeing that no living human being

Ever yet was blessed with seeing bird above his chamber door—

Bird or beast upon the sculptured bust above his chamber door,

                With such a name as "Nevermore."

Je m'émerveillai fort d'entendre ce disgracieux volatile s'énoncer aussi clairement,

Quoique sa réponse n'eût que peu de sens et peu d'à-propos;

Car on ne peut s'empêcher de convenir que nul homme vivant

N'eût encore l'heur de voir un oiseau au-dessus de la porte de sa chambre—

Un oiseau ou toute autre bête sur le buste sculpté, au-dessus de la porte de sa chambre,

                Avec un nom tel que: « Jamais plus. »

But the Raven, sitting lonely on that placid bust, spoke only

That one word, as if his soul in that one word he did outpour.

Nothing further then he uttered; not a feather then he fluttered—

Till I scarcely more than muttered, "Other friends have flown before—

On the morrow he will leave me, as my Hopes have flown before."

>Then the bird said, "Nevermore."

Mais le Corbeau, perché solitairement sur ce buste placide,

Parla ce seul mot comme si, son âme, en ce seul mot, il la répandait.

Je ne proférai donc rien de plus: il n'agita donc pas de plume—

Jusqu'à ce que je fis à peine davantage que marmotter « D'autres amis déjà ont pris leur vol—

Demain il me laissera comme mes Espérances déjà ont pris leur vol. »

>*Alors l'oiseau dit: « Jamais plus. »*

Startled at the stillness broken by reply so aptly spoken,

"Doubtless," said I, "what it utters is its only stock and store,

Caught from some unhappy master, whom unmerciful Disaster

Followed fast and followed faster till his songs one burden bore—

Till the dirges of his Hope the melancholy burden bore

>Of 'Never—nevermore.'"

Tressaillant au calme rompu par une réplique si bien parlée:

« Sans doute dis-je, ce qu'il profère est tout son fonds et son bagage,

Pris à quelque malheureux maître que l'impitoyable Désastre

Suivit de près et de très-près suivit jusqu'à ce que ses chansons comportassent un unique refrain—

Jusqu'à ce que les chants funèbres de son Espérance comportassent le mélancolique refrain

>*De « Jamais—jamais plus. »*

But the Raven still beguiling all my sad soul into smiling,

Straight I wheeled a cushioned seat in front of bird and bust and door;

Then, upon the velvet sinking, I betook myself to linking

Fancy unto fancy, thinking what this ominous bird of yore—

What this grim, ungainly, ghastly, gaunt and ominous bird of yore

> Meant in croaking "Nevermore."

Le Corbeau induisant toute ma triste âme encore au sourire,

Je roulai soudain un siège à coussins en face de l'oiseau et du buste et de la porte;

Et m'enfonçant dans le velours, je me pris à enchaîner

Songerie à songerie, pensant à ce que cet augural oiseau de jadis—

A ce que ce sombre, disgracieux, sinistre, maigre et augural oiseau de jadis

> *Signifiait en croassant: « Jamais plus. »*

This I sat engaged in guessing, but no syllable expressing

To the fowl whose fiery eyes now burned into my bosom's core;

This and more I sat divining, with my head at ease reclining

On the cushion's velvet lining that the lamp-light gloated o'er,

But whose velvet violet lining with the lamp-light gloating o'er,

>   She shall press, ah, nevermore!

Cela, je m'assis occupé à le conjecturer, mais n'adressant pas une syllabe

A l'oiseau dont les yeux de feu brûlaient, maintenant, au fond de mon sein;

Cela et plus encore, je m'assis pour le deviner, ma tête reposant à l'aise

Sur la housse de velours des coussins que dévorait la lumière de la lampe,

Housse violette de velours dévoré par la lumière de la lampe,

>   *Qu'Elle ne pressera plus, ah! jamais plus.*

Then, me thought, the air grew denser, perfumed from an unseen censer,

Swung by Seraphim whose foot-falls tinkled on the tufted floor.

"Wretch," I cried, "thy God hath lent thee—by these angels he hath sent thee

Respite—respite and nepenthe from thy memories of Lenore!

Quaff, oh quaff this kind nepenthe, and forget this lost Lenore!"

       Quoth the Raven, "Nevermore."

L'air, me sembla-t-il, devint alors plus dense, parfumé selon un encensoir invisible,

Balancé par les Séraphins dont le pied, dans sa chute, tintait sur l'étoffe du parquet.

« Misérable, m'écriai-je, ton Dieu t'a prêté—il t'a envoyé, par ces anges,

Le répit—le répit et le népenthès dans ta mémoire de Lénore !

Bois ! oh ! bois ce bon népenthès et oublie cette Lénore perdue! »

Le Corbeau dit: « Jamais plus! »

"Prophet!" said I, "thing of evil!—prophet still, if bird or devil!—

Whether Tempter sent, or whether tempest tossed thee here ashore,

Desolate yet all undaunted, on this desert land enchanted—

On this home by Horror haunted—tell me truly, I implore—

Is there—is there balm in Gilead?—tell me—tell me, I implore!"

                    Quoth the Raven, "Nevermore."

« Prophète, dis-je, être de malheur! prophète, oui, oiseau ou démon ! —

Que si le Tentateur t'envoya ou la tempête t'échoua vers ces bords,

Désolé et encore tout indompté, vers cette déserte terre enchantée—

Vers ce logis par l'horreur hanté: dis-moi véritablement, je t'implore ! —

Y a-t-il du baume en Judée ?—dis-moi, je t'implore ! »

                    Le Corbeau dit: « Jamais plus ! »

"Prophet!" said I, "thing of evil!—prophet still, if bird or devil!

By that Heaven that bends above us—by that God we both adore—

Tell this soul with sorrow laden if, within the distant Aidenn,

It shall clasp a saintly maiden whom the angels name Lenore—

Clasp a rare and radiant maiden whom the angels name Lenore."

                        Quoth the Raven, "Nevermore."

« Prophète, dis-je, être de malheur! prophète, oui, oiseau ou démon !

Par les Cieux sur nous épars—et le Dieu que nous adorons tous deux—

Dis à cette âme de chagrin chargée si, dans le distant Eden,

Elle doit embrasser une jeune fille sanctifiée que les anges nomment Lénore—

Embrasser une rare et rayonnante jeune fille que les anges nomment Lénore. »

Le Corbeau dit: « Jamais plus ! »

"Be that word our sign of parting, bird or fiend!" I shrieked, upstarting—

"Get thee back into the tempest and the Night's Plutonian shore!

Leave no black plume as a token of that lie thy soul hath spoken!

Leave my loneliness unbroken!—quit the bust above my door!

Take thy beak from out my heart, and take thy form from off my door!"

Quoth the Raven, "Nevermore."

« Que ce mot soit le signal de notre séparation, oiseau ou malin esprit, » hurlai-je, en me dressant—

« Recule en la tempête et le rivage plutonien de Nuit !

Ne laisse pas une plume noire ici comme un gage du mensonge qu'a proféré ton âme.

Laisse inviolé mon abandon ! quitte le buste au-dessus de ma porte !

Ôte ton bec de mon cœur et jette ta forme loin de ma porte ! »

Le Corbeau dit: « Jamais plus ! »

And the Raven, never flitting, still is sitting—still is sitting

On the pallid bust of Pallas just above my chamber door;

And his eyes have all the seeming of a Demon's that is dreaming,

And the lamp-light o'er him streaming throws his shadow on the floor;

And my soul from out that shadow that lies floating on the floor

Shall be lifted—nevermore!

Et le Corbeau, sans voleter, siége encore—siége encore

Sur le buste pallide de Pallas, juste au-dessus de la porte de ma chambre,

Et ses yeux ont toute la semblance des yeux d'un démon qui rêve,

Et la lumière de la lampe, ruisselant sur lui, projette son ombre à terre:

Et mon âme, de cette ombre qui gît flottante à terre,

Ne s'élèvera—jamais plus !

ILLUSTRATIONS PAR GUSTAVE DORÉ

ILLUSTRATION 1 TITLE-PAGE, DESIGNED BY ELIHU VEDDER.

ILLUSTRATIONS

ILLUSTRATION 2 "NEVERMORE."

Illustration 3 ANANKE.

ILLUSTRATION 4 "ONCE UPON A MIDNIGHT DREARY, WHILE I PONDERED, WEAK AND WEARY, OVER MANY A QUAINT AND CURIOUS VOLUME OF FORGOTTEN LORE."

ILLUSTRATION 5 "AH, DISTINCTLY I REMEMBER IT WAS IN THE BLEAK DECEMBER,
AND EACH SEPARATE DYING EMBER WROUGHT ITS GHOST UPON THE FLOOR."

ILLUSTRATION 6 "EAGERLY I WISHED THE MORROW;—VAINLY I HAD SOUGHT TO BORROW FROM MY BOOKS SURCEASE OF SORROW—SORROW FOR THE LOST LENORE."

ILLUSTRATION 7 "SORROW FOR THE LOST LENORE."

ILLUSTRATION 8 "FOR THE RARE AND RADIANT MAIDEN WHOM THE ANGELS NAME LENORE— NAMELESS HERE FOR EVERMORE."

ILLUSTRATION 9 "'T IS SOME VISITER ENTREATING ENTRANCE AT MY CHAMBER DOOR—
SOME LATE VISITER ENTREATING ENTRANCE AT MY CHAMBER DOOR."

ILLUSTRATION 10 "HERE I OPENED WIDE THE DOOR;—
DARKNESS THERE, AND NOTHING MORE."

ILLUSTRATION 11 "DOUBTING, DREAMING DREAMS NO MORTAL EVER DARED TO DREAM BEFORE."

ILLUSTRATION 12 "'SURELY,' SAID I, 'SURELY THAT IS SOMETHING AT MY WINDOW LATTICE; LET ME SEE, THEN, WHAT THEREAT IS, AND THIS MYSTERY EXPLORE.'"

ILLUSTRATION 13 "OPEN HERE I FLUNG THE SHUTTER."

ILLUSTRATION 14. "A STATELY RAVEN OF THE SAINTLY DAYS OF YORE.
NOT THE LEAST OBEISANCE MADE HE; NOT A MINUTE STOPPED OR STAYED HE."

ILLUSTRATION 15 "PERCHED UPON A BUST OF PALLAS
JUST ABOVE MY CHAMBER DOOR—
PERCHED, AND SAT, AND NOTHING MORE."

ILLUSTRATIONS

ILLUSTRATION 16 "WANDERING FROM THE NIGHTLY SHORE."

ILLUSTRATION 17 "TILL I SCARCELY MORE THAN MUTTERED, 'OTHER FRIENDS HAVE FLOWN BEFORE— ON THE MORROW HE WILL LEAVE ME, AS MY HOPES HAVE FLOWN BEFORE.'"

ILLUSTRATION 18 "THEN, UPON THE VELVET SINKING, I BETOOK MYSELF TO LINKING FANCY UNTO FANCY."

Illustration 19 "But whose velvet violet lining with the lamplight gloating o'er

She shall press, ah, nevermore!"

ILLUSTRATION 20 "'WRETCH,' I CRIED, 'THY GOD HATH LENT THEE—BY THESE ANGELS HE HATH SENT THEE
RESPITE—RESPITE AND NEPENTHE FROM THY MEMORIES OF LENORE!'"

Illustration 21 "On this home by Horror haunted."

ILLUSTRATION 22 . . . . "TELL ME TRULY, I IMPLORE—
IS THERE—IS THERE BALM IN GILEAD?—TELL ME—
TELL ME, I IMPLORE!"

ILLUSTRATION 23 "TELL THIS SOUL WITH SORROW LADEN IF, WITHIN THE DISTANT AIDENN, IT SHALL CLASP A SAINTED MAIDEN WHOM THE ANGELS NAME LENORE."

ILLUSTRATION 24 "'BE THAT WORD OUR SIGN OF PARTING, BIRD OR FIEND!' I SHRIEKED, UPSTARTING."

ILLUSTRATION 25 "'GET THEE BACK INTO THE TEMPEST AND THE NIGHT'S PLUTONIAN SHORE!'"

ILLUSTRATION 26 "AND MY SOUL FROM OUT THAT SHADOW THAT LIES FLOATING ON THE FLOOR SHALL BE LIFTED—NEVERMORE!"

Illustration 27 The secret of the Sphinx.

Made in United States
North Haven, CT
13 December 2021

12680987R00035